Amazing Raptors

Written by Catherine Baker

Collins

Winged predators

Birds of **prey** are also
called raptors.
These amazing creatures
are the top **predators**
of the sky.

They catch and eat smaller animals and birds.

3

Look closer ...

Every part of this bald eagle helps it catch prey.

huge wings save
energy when flying

laser-sharp sight

curved beak
rips meat

powerful claws
carry large prey

5

Where do raptors live?

Raptors are found all over the world.

Barn owls and ospreys live on every continent but Antarctica!

Barn owls live in forests, fields and towns.

Ospreys live by coasts and lakes.

7

Gigantic raptor

The world's biggest raptor is the Andean condor.

Its **wingspan** is over three metres. It weighs as much as a three-year-old child!

9

Tiny but deadly

The smallest raptor is
the black-thighed falconet.
It weighs about as much
as a packet of crisps!

10

It eats mostly insects, including butterflies.

This kind of falcon is not only the fastest raptor –
it's the fastest creature on Earth!

When it dives, it hurtles at about the speed of a Formula 1 car.

Endangered raptors

White-rumped vultures were once common.
But thousands died from eating food
containing harmful chemicals.

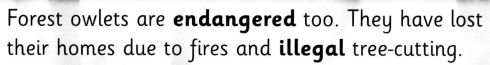

Forest owlets are **endangered** too. They have lost their homes due to fires and **illegal** tree-cutting.

Strangest-looking raptor?

Most raptors look amazing – but is this
the strangest of all?

Secretary birds live in Africa. They catch prey by chasing it on foot!

Where to see raptors

Look out for raptors near you. You may see them ...

... flying overhead

... perching on chimneys

... or at a display!

Glossary

endangered at risk of dying out

illegal against the law

predators animals that hunt and kill other animals

prey animal killed for food by other animals

wingspan length of wings from tip to tip

Amazing raptors!

After reading

Letters and Sounds: Phase 5

Word count: 288

Focus phonemes: /igh/ y, ie /ee/ y, e, ey, e-e /j/ g, ge /ai/ a, eigh /ch/ t, tch /v/ ve /oo/ u /w/ wh /c/ ch /l/ le

Common exception words: of, to, the, are, do, were, once, their

Curriculum links: Science: Animals, including humans

National Curriculum learning objectives: Reading/word reading: apply phonic knowledge and skills as the route to decode words, read other words of more than one syllable that contain taught GPCs; read words containing common suffixes; Reading/comprehension: drawing on what they already know or on background information and vocabulary provided by the teacher

Developing fluency

- Your child may enjoy hearing you read the book.
- Take turns to read a page of text. Check your child notices and pauses at the commas on pages 6, 11 and 13. Check they also pause for the dash on pages 12 and 16, and the ellipses (pages 4, 18 and 19).

Phonic practice

- Point to **creature** on page 12. Challenge your child to separate the syllables as they sound out the word. (*crea-ture*)
- Repeat for **endangered** on page 15. Challenge them to separate the syllables as they sound out the word. (*en-dang-ered*)
- Take turns to find other long words with more than one syllable to point to and sound out.

Extending vocabulary

- Ask your child to think of a synonym (word or words of similar meaning) for these words ending in -ing. Ask them to check their meaning in context first.

  page 2 amazing (e.g. *incredible, astonishing*)
  page 14 eating (e.g. *swallowing, consuming*)
  page 17 chasing (e.g. *following, hunting*)
- Take turns to think of another -ing word for the other to suggest a synonym.